Prognosis

ALSO BY JIM MOORE

The New Body
What the Bird Sees
How We Missed Belgium (with Deborah Keenan)
Minnesota Writes: Poetry (coeditor)
The Freedom of History
The Long Experience of Love
Writing with Tagore: Homages and Variations
Lightning at Dinner
What It's Like Here
Invisible Strings
Underground: New and Selected Poems

Prognosis

POEMS

Jim Moore

Graywolf Press

This publication is made possible, in part, by the voters of Minnesota through a Minnesota State Arts Board Operating Support grant, thanks to a legislative appropriation from the arts and cultural heritage fund. Significant support has also been provided by Target Foundation, the McKnight Foundation, the Lannan Foundation, the Amazon Literary Partnership, and other generous contributions from foundations, corporations, and individuals. To these organizations and individuals we offer our heartfelt thanks.

Published by Graywolf Press
250 Third Avenue North, Suite 600
Minneapolis, Minnesota 55401

www.graywolfpress.org

Published in the United States of America
Printed in Canada

ISBN 978-1-64445-070-3

2 4 6 8 9 7 5 3 1
First Graywolf Printing, 2021

Library of Congress Control Number: 2020951329

Cover design: Kyle G. Hunter
Cover photo © JoAnn Verburg, 1975, untitled (detail from a triptych)

FOR JOANN

CONTENTS

Prognosis

LOOK AGAIN

for Chantz Erolin and Marie Howe

It was just luck: orange groves,

those two olive orchards, the way

we sat side by side on the picnic bench.

You in that white blouse, open

at the throat. Those goats in the pen

with the two dogs who looked outnumbered,

but happy in their confusion. A gun mistaken

for a taser. A murder. You know

the rest. None of it is just luck.

Too early for the swallows, but right on time

for the red-winged blackbirds. Look away,

then look back. I can almost see it,

the world as it really is. But not quite.

*

AND

I
realize my mistake only now:
all I needed to do
that day twenty years ago
was be with my friend
who called out,
"But I don't want to die."
To stand even closer by his side.
To just be there.
Admit into my life
all that longing.

WHATEVER ELSE

Whatever else, the little smile on the face of the woman
listening to a music the rest of us can't hear and a sky at dawn
with a moon all its own. Whatever else, the construction crane
high above us waiting to be told how to do our bidding,
we who bid and bid and bid. Whatever else, the way cook #1
looks with such longing at cook #2. Let's not be too sad
about how sad we are. I know about the disappearance
of the river dolphins, the sea turtles with tumors.
I know about the way the dead
don't return no matter how long they take to die
in the back of the police car. I know about the thousand ways our world
betrays itself. Whatever else, my friend spreading wide his arms,
looks out at the river and says,
"After all, what choice did I have?" After all,
I saw the man walking who'd had the stroke, saw the woman
whose body won't stop shaking. I saw the frog in the tall grass,
boldly telling us who truly matters. I saw the world
proclaim itself an unlit vesper candle while a crow
flew into the tip of it, sleek black match, burning.

ALSO KNOWN AS

If you are closer to being old
than you would like to be and slowness
begins to redefine the idea of difficulty
into something you would much rather
take a pass on, then it is time for the sky
to grow larger than the earth, than the sea even.
You need to go to that place where your story
is seriously quiet. Nothing in it counts
compared to the things sky
calls out to: birds, clouds, the occasional cypress
that has reached beyond itself.
You could call it a kind of waiting
and that would be fair. There is a green bench
in the sky—a corner of heaven, you could say—
and there you can sit in the shade
and watch the grandfather and grandson walk by.
The little one makes the older one laugh
again and again and that is the way it works
in heaven. Also known as going home.
Also known as getting over yourself.

LAST DAY AT SEVENTY-FIVE

Summer Solstice, 2018

I did finally arrive. What a surprise:

not to sing the song of creation, but to be sung by it.

The pine trees smelling faintly of pine trees.

Shadows in all the right places.

Loneliness and oleander

vying for my attention.

Purple weeds in the long grass.

The smell of the linden trees. Crows and sea gulls:

all their dire warnings.

Meanwhile, the light goes on and on.

CHEESE, ALMONDS, EGGS

He'd been sick only five days. Our friend.
It turned out later maybe it was the virus,
maybe a heart attack. An autopsy
was refused to him. No one
will ever know. Now he is ash.

Soon the grocery store will open.
Because I am old I will go in first.
Cheese, almonds, eggs if they have them.
I can't think any further than that.
Yesterday, I heard the first
red-winged blackbird. We were on the bridge
where they come back every year
to the tall weeds by the river.

A small invisible wind
that doesn't know what to do
with itself, like a child
lost somewhere near home,
but too far away for him to see
how to make his way back.
If you tell me, *Try to rest*, I will say
I am trying to find the words to say
how it feels to be that child:
I know no other way to rest.

INSTEAD

It was not promised to me to write a poem for the ages.
        Not promised, happiness like a path
down to a river, sloping gently,

carrying me along. Not promised, the peace
        that passeth all understanding.
Instead, I was promised rain on an empty street

in a provincial city far away
        from the center of power.
Promised red gerania under an overhang,

headlights on a distant bluff, trees in wind
        bearing up,
as if born for it as dancers are born

for the warm-ups as much as for the performance.
        Born to see the small boy carrying an umbrella,
holding the hand of his hatless father. Yes, that.

Reconciliation
        was never the point. Nor the violence
emanating from the capitol.

This world is the only home for those who thought not
        a thing in the world mattered as much
as their sorrow. There is a way to hide

and still be found. There is a stillness
        which begins only after the final mourner
has left the church.

BE THEM NOW

June 17, 2015
Charleston, South Carolina
Venice, Sestiere Sant'Elena

Be an earthworm pushing the dirt around on Sant'Elena.
Be those boys playing volleyball: spike and shout.
Drop to your knee when they drop to their knees.
Pound the red earth as they do, then fall laughing on your back.
Now be the ancient Italian in the fedora, leaning on his cane:
is he the stillness of the universe?

Be the ragged cypresses at the edge of the lagoon, the mother calling
    out inside you.

Be him again, the young man you were in 1970
standing under barbed wire. Your friend said,
"No matter how long you live you will always be White."

Be the whole day falling into night.

Be them now: The sea, the mountains, the locusts, the lagoon.
The cypress needles growing, the cypress needles strewn, the
    privileged one.
The boats. The dogs. The light shadowed, the light bare.
The labor of the man pushing the cart filled with dirty sheets.
The silver foil matted in the grass. The roses by the bench. The ticket
    booth.

> *Knowing you will be shot*
> *Knowing you will be the one after next.*
> *Knowing you will be next.*
> *Knowing   it is now.*

Be the locusts, be the locusts, be the locusts.

Be everyone and everything: the sky full of lightning,
the mother nursing by the lagoon, that soldier
with an ornamental sword, a building in ruins,
city half-disappeared in clouded moonlight.
Be those trees darkened with twilight, dark as shrouds.
Be the baby dazed with milk.
Be the shawl shielding the mother's breasts.

Two dogs lie panting in the grass.
Be the next vaporetto approaching. Motor slowing. Almost here now.

Be now a breathing son about to step on deck.
Be a spared daughter.
Be them now: the ones who sail away.

ODE TO MY KIND

Here I am, once again among my kind,
half-moon high outside the window
rowing its light down the empty street, parting
the dark waves of the parking lot, soaking the oak leaves
all the way through. Coffee shop at Broadway and Central,
no booth, perched on a stool and counting
on making it through the night.

Everyone plenty younger, yes, but still
my kind, hunched over and frowning
at computers, at phones, at paper with words crossed out,
everyone busy making marks or marking time.
We like to laugh, heads thrown back, and sometimes we bury
those heads in our arms and cry. We like to exclaim
Birds! when birds there suddenly are;
ditto, *Moon!* as if never before had anyone seen
such a thing.

October 2018, miserable, miserable
year swirling all around us,
swindling us out of joy, and yet:
there are these birds calling out,
birds and half-moon
to guide me through the darkness, in a country
that reels and staggers like a drunk father
who has run over his own child in the driveway
and wants somehow to cover it up,
to bury the child behind the house.
Maybe no one will ever know how bad it is.
But we know, my kind,
and we sit, holding coffee, or maybe even
holding someone's hand, maybe writing about
how the sorrow never ends,

only one hour until closing time,
sixty minutes left to try to figure out
how to bear the unbearable,
knowing we are so close to the end.
Then tomorrow, damned if we don't
show up all over again,
because that's what we do,
heads bent to the task at hand:
Birds! Moon! Ruin!

THINGS THAT KEEP ME FROM FORGETTING WHO I AM:

It has come to this: everywhere I go, I go slowly.

* * *

Spring, spring, spring, do it to me again.

* * *

A country that kills easily. A country that refuses the starving. A country that . . . well, you know the rest.

* * *

Years of the darkened room, flat on my back, eyes closed. And now? A glass of water, April clouds.

* * *

We'll walk today, my friend and I, along the river. His sadness and mine, different, but when we laugh we laugh together.

* * *

Let's go to a movie. Pass the popcorn, pass the chocolate, pass me a blood orange, please, from the blood orange tree.

* * *

It's settled then: I'll sit by the monument to the fallen for as long as it takes.

*

. . . and the light in trees,
which Virginia Woolf
called a "buried treasure."
For example, Juanita
in her wheelchair being
pushed for the last time
by George down Main
in the sunlight, face
tilted up, eyes closed,
calling out, "Get me
the fucking marijuana!"

IT WAS GIVEN TO ME

Saw by the light of the blue bridge

    and the shadows swallows make

        first thing at dawn.

Saw by the fallen rain

    and the four streetlights

        lined up in a row. There is a truth

a bare branch knows

    in winter, nakedness

        under moonlight, twenty

below zero

    and growing colder.

        I know that truth, too.

Probably

    I was alone too much

        in this life.

Probably

    children with names

        I had given them

would have helped,

     a girl of seven

          buttoning her father's shirt

one stop higher

     so no one else can see the chest

          she loves.

Still and all, to me it was given

     to see these swallows, claimed

          by an unearthly light at dawn, unencumbered

by thoughts of what might have been.

GRACE

Fra Angelico

In Cosmo de Medici's cell
there is a fresco where everyone is waiting in line
to kneel at the feet of the newly born God.
At the end of the line, one bearded man
rests his cheek against the muzzle of his horse,
waiting patiently to see God the baby,
lying there on the ground, ready to be loved.
Perhaps holding him will feel like
holding the hand of my friend
in the hospital who no longer speaks except
for three words: *Yes*, *God*, and *Tree*,
as she strokes my wrist unceasingly.

THE PANDEMIC HALO

The pandemic halo began to appear a few weeks into it.
Oddly, the first time, it was surrounding the head
of an old lab. He was being walked, as usual, at 7 a.m.
by his young owner. Lots of lamppost stops. There it was:
faint at first, then hovering at a tilt above the silky head.

I thought maybe it was a weird trick of light—the day
was bright—but the next morning it was still there.
That same day, the nurse who wears a pink cape and parks
in the lot across from me, almost always empty now, was trotting along
on her way to the clinic that is just below my window. She had it, too.

I don't think she noticed it at all. She was walking quickly, a little late
to work, so I think that was on her mind, not holiness.
The third day a young man in a red cap with a backpack slouched past.
I had never seen him before. You could see he was seriously depressed,
looking down at the sidewalk. But it was there, firmly in place.

It was above him, of course; he couldn't see how beautiful
he really was. That woman with the nasty little dog: same thing.
By now the pandemic halo is well recorded. Everyone knows about it.
We almost take it for granted, what had once seemed amazing.
Somehow it is related to breath. When we die it goes away.

After the pandemic is over they say the halo effect will disappear.
They say we will return to life as usual. We won't need it,
they say. I have my doubts. I think we might need it more than ever.
I think we might be saying things like, "Remember how amazing it was
during the pandemic, how everyone had a halo, how grief and holiness
    were all
we knew of the world and the sight of a dog at a lamppost could bring
    us to tears?"

TRANSFIGURATION

Variation on Li Po

It's graveland time for the soldier
who used to make wine for us.
He's someplace now where dawn
never cuts the long night short.
He doesn't need to shake his hair loose anymore,
doesn't need to play at teasing her,
that mother of his who mourned him
even while he was alive, still more now
that he won't ever come home late again,
calling out to her casually, the way he does.

CANNOT SLEEP

for Ping Chong with lines from Du Fu

Last night,
dinner with an old friend.
At the end,
after talking of the collapse
of our country,
"Send me one of those Chinese poems,
one you really love," he says,
then hood up,
he is gone into the darkness.

I cannot sleep
plagued by thoughts of war,
and powerless
to spare the world its fate.

This morning, men keep climbing
an outside staircase. Slowly,
slowly, one after the other,
up the side of a building
newly condemned.

Obviously,
we must bend our heads
and cry.
Though sometimes the city
shines beautifully
from this high above,
a toy
newly out of the box.

Soon, you will come home.
Soon, chickpeas, fennel, tomatoes, couscous,
　　　the walk over the bridge
to the other side of the river
　　　where once a group of us stood for hours
guarding a giant snapping turtle
　　　who had come to a construction site
to lay her eggs, but then stopped
　　　in the middle of the road.
She refused to move until finally
　　　she remembered there was a river
to which she belonged and very slowly
　　　made her way toward home.

THINGS THAT KEEP ME FROM FORGETTING WHO I AM:

Sitting right here where the reckless world begins.

* * *

Someone sick is being carried away very fast in an ambulance that passes two girls in the park combing each other's hair.

* * *

The eagle perched above, the river far below, the heart permanently broken, the small stone wall falling apart, the weeds in the cracks of the wall, and everything else, Mother, that you missed in your unhappiness.

* * *

Getting old and saying too much about it. Oh, well.

*

... and later, back home,
the dog and I watch how
the October snow falls
like a dream of snow.
We go for deep sighs
and nodding off at the foot
of a strange universe together
in a warm room. An unknown voice
outside the door and the dog growls a bit.
When she was a puppy
she would have barked.
Now she just turns toward me,
making sure I notice it, too:
the strangeness of this world.

NOT TO KNOW HOW TO LIVE

       All modesty is false modesty
when it comes to poems,
       or to the silence
in which poems begin
       before they are words,
when they are still daisies
       at the foot of a dead god
in an anonymous painting,
       thirteenth century. Not to know how to live
is one thing, and nothing
       to be ashamed of.
But not to know
       how to sit in front of those daisies
with tears in my eyes:
       what a waste that would be.

That man running

along the river
    wishes he were anyone
but who he is.
        Even the man he was yesterday
would do, the man who heard
    the train whistle
from the viaduct above him,
        then felt the trembling
of the world all the way through.
        Yes, that man would do.

MY BRACELET

for Peggy Berg

There is sunlight and a staircase ending at the sky. There are electrical wires, a black cable. Then the sound of the train going away. There is my bracelet made of jasper that Peggy made for me. For decades she has known sorrow and beauty. There are mountains and forest fires. Lives that might have lived through her, but didn't. Lives that do still live through her. There is the river and the sweetness of going down to the river. There is all that darkness rushing under the arches of the old stone bridge. The waiting darkness. The patience. There is the going away: let's get that straight once and for all. And the new waitress, her hand shaking, the tattoo pulsing at her neck, which reads, *And stray impassioned in the littering leaves.*

TODAY'S MEDITATION

The day I was released from prison there was fog, then sunshine.
It was fall. The leaves were changing. I went for a walk in the dark
with the woman I loved. I wrote a postcard to my friend,
still in jail. "I'm free!" was all it said. It was true, too,
in that one moment. The woman touched me.
We stood together under the old trees outside the brick house
where the rest of my family waited for me to come in from the darkness
and become one of them again. Yesterday,
under the railroad bridge, I saw
the homeless woman who plays the violin.
She was wearing her red bandanna, unhappy
as always. Still, she managed a smile.
When she began to play I stood and listened.
At first it was politeness
that kept me there. How hard she tried,
how off-key she remained.
Above us on the bridge a train
went dragging and squealing by,
putting an end to her concert. We stood there
a moment more, listening to the way coal sounds
when it's fast on its way somewhere else,
our bodies shaking a little from the vibration,
as if something dark and uncountable
were passing through us. Then we nodded,
one to the other, as humans do
when something has been accomplished in us,
though we couldn't say exactly what.

IN THE POEMS I LOVE

In the poems I love
    there are sailboats
        taking lonely Chinese poets away

from other lonely Chinese poets,
    and from willow trees
        along the shore,

barely rooted.
    Such clarity in the poems
        I love, such mystery.

And when dawn comes at last
    after a long restless night
        in the poems I love,

sometimes the poet will reveal,
    with much relief, how small
        we really are.

For a moment the poem stalls
    while the poet laughs, thinks
to contrast the calm of the sky

to the unfairness of the universe,
    a comparison which implies, without
        saying a word,

the loneliness of it all.
    In the poems I love,
        no one is ever accused

of taking the curve
　　　　by the cemetery too quickly,
　　　　　　　or of overelaborating

in the second stanza
　　　　and no one is ever judged too lonely
　　　　　　　for his own good. If it weren't

for loneliness we might not need
　　　　to see the way a crow finally settles
　　　　　　　on the top of a streetlight,

and stays still so long there,
　　　　just waiting for us to get it,
　　　　　　　how ridiculously easy life is,

alit like this. And it's no small thing
　　　　to have seen the crow
　　　　　　　in his sleek indifference,

his black pool
　　　　of unruffledness,
　　　　　　　how he flew away, rising

all at once, not a trace of him remaining:
　　　　only the streetlight shining,
　　　　　　　illuminating a small patch of darkness

in the poems I love.

Driving the River Road

past the bridge where all those years ago
      my teacher jumped.
Tonight: fog, a warm wind,
      people with umbrellas
hurrying from one place to the next.

PANDEMIC PSALM

May 2020, and none of us is thinking all that straight.
Sometimes these days we say *psalm* and *amen*
when what we really mean is
we always wanted to believe we were not
the be-all and end-all, and now, for sure,
we know.

THINGS THAT KEEP ME FROM FORGETTING
WHO I AM:

Wishing only to be loved by everyone in this café. Is it too much to ask?

* * *

Red-winged blackbird crying out from his light pole and I am running across a bridge as if it actually matters to get to the other side.

* * *

Grain elevators, bare branches, these four gray smokestacks: my life.

* * *

The woman I barely know and I stand together a moment in the crowded café, speaking of her daughter who is in trouble, but maybe doing better. When we say goodbye we hug. It is 6 p.m. and there is still light in the sky. Not happiness exactly, but the residue of her kindness stays with me on the short walk home in the last of the light.

*

. . . and the turquoise sky.
This loneliness: no, it
won't go away. Now
the first star. Now the red
lights, blinking
on top of the towers.
When all is said
and done, it's always
the right time to set out alone,
having felt, even if only a little,
what it might mean to die, then to go on
living by the light of death,
happy, stained with longing,
hurrying down the waxed hallway
toward the prison library.

I call it joy

this being unnoticed. Sitting like this
        next to the stone lamb outside the cathedral.
My lost soul, which prefers the stone lamb
        to the living God. Prefers these deep shadows
to the summer day. The way he took me
        all those years ago, shattered me
so that fifty-seven years later, I might sit
        next to the smoothness of this stone lamb,
know the stone joy of being unnoticed.
        People go in the cathedral all day long,
visiting their God on their knees. That man
        who betrayed me when I was a boy,
first held me up to a tree so I would know
        what smell lemon blossoms have.

THE PROBLEM

"You can't have everything," they say. But the problem is
you do. On quiet days, according to Bellini, each face is filled
with its own death, quietly nearby
like an old friend who knows how to remain silent.
And then there are the chalky white roads
that wind through the distance in his paintings,
barely visible at dusk, roads that run all the way to the edge
of the frame, then stop. We can go no farther. Our hearts stop with them,
cry out, cannot be consoled: and that, too, is having everything.

MAYBE THIS HAPPENS ALMOST EVERY DAY
OF MY LIFE

Maybe it's like the time I got off the boat by mistake,
the wrong island in Greece at twenty-two. Tinos. Midnight.
An empty harbor café. Also afraid.
Maybe this happens almost every day in my life.
Getting off at the wrong island again and again.
That same loneliness. The old woman in the black dress
is there at the harbor, waiting for someone in need.
She leads me to a dark room, brings cold water in a bucket.
I drink, it, too, for the night is long, and I am still so very thirsty.

ADMIT IT

A man in a mask and wearing a fat tank on his back is bent at the door
  of the parking garage.
He is spraying and wiping, wiping and spraying. Another man with no
  mask and no hair shuffle-dances around him,
gives a wave, crosses the street, tries to open the door to the hotel,
  which is locked and closed, darkened for good:
OK, now what? He turns and walks back toward the parking garage.
  The man with the tank doesn't look up,
he's all about the door handle now, rubbing it again and again. The
  bald man is past waving.
He's not happy. He looks down and away. Admit it, it's always been
  just a little too hard
to live. Here comes the doctor who works in the clinic downstairs. She
  wears a laminated name tag
and carries a big bag. Maybe it has masks in it, maybe oxygen tanks.
  She limps as she walks. The bag is too heavy
and she is in too much of a rush. It's nearly 8 a.m. I bet her first patient
  comes in at 8. I bet he'll have
complaints, but try to put a good face on it all. There was a saint once,
  tenth century, who suggested
we do nothing but look into our own hearts and say what we see there.
  I see fear, hope, despair, and need.
Sometimes I'm older than anyone in the world and one foot is out
  the door, sometimes I'm a baby six months old
and my mother is swinging me back and forth like a small sack
  of potatoes and I am laughing so hard I can hardly bear having
  been born.

SPOLETO

Piazza #1—empty buildings, spiderwebs, broken windows.

Piazza #2—hundreds of teenagers at midnight, some drunk and stoned, some eating pistachio ice cream.

Piazza #3—old people: canes, bent heads, green benches.

Elsewhere: pine trees and cedars; cats sliding along stone walls, scooting under cars.

From the city wall you can see the whole valley, plus clouds and stars and the lit cross on the mountain.

An ambulance goes by—the shock of its siren.

One of the teenagers runs out of Piazza #2 in tears: goes to the fountain by the cedar tree and buries her head for a moment in the living water.

GREED

I take what I can get from the time I have left.
A grasping way to live, I know, but it's what I've got.

In the daytime, cicadas. At night, crickets and tree frogs.
Late summer, poppies: more orange than red.

I drink from the ancient fountain that carries water down
from the ancient mountain. I sit on a stone ledge
waiting for the woman I love. I need and need and need.

Pine needles strewn
all over the grass smelling of sunlight
and sacrifice, as if burned at the altar.

The grass itself,
the grandfather and grandmother each
pushing a stroller, oh, the happiness
of a duty gladly assumed.

                    Poem,
don't abandon me to what I already know.
I'm like an empty stroller in search of its child.
                    Or
the Mother-to-be of God being told by Fra Angelico's angel,
I've got some good news and some bad news.

It's a sickness to be her. To be struck dumb
with sanctity. To know you cannot manage such a thing
without more pain than can be borne.

                    And yet,
you will bear it because that's what you do.

Hey, look over here!
I'm that boy hiding under the lilac bush
behind the clothesline,
in the dusty summer shadow: someone
keeps calling me in a loud voice, someone desperate for me to
come home right now.

THINGS THAT KEEP ME FROM FORGETTING
WHO I AM:

Whatever else to say about life, certainly say this: it was too much.

* * *

Just the two of us in a little motel room, surrounded by pure Nebraska.

* * *

After hitting my own ear on the car door at 10 p.m., fell asleep: stupid, hurting, in love.

* * *

Feeling bad about feeling bad, nevertheless, I still refuse to eat my half of the rotten banana.

* * *

"What's the meaning of life?" you ask, completely seriously, then do 100 sit-ups as I sit there watching.

* * *

Mother India, late at night, Omaha, four friends, at least two of whom are afraid of death, eating basmati rice, laughing, while on the radio lost souls try to explain to lost souls why being a lost soul is the best.

* * *

Whatever else to say about life, certainly say this: it was never enough.

*

. . . and looking at the saints
lined up on the staircase—
Giotto saints—what gets me
(even like this, as postcards)
is how calm their faces are,
and how alive. It is a fierce calm
that demands: but demands what?
I remember, forty years ago,
the young woman reading
George Eliot on the bus to Chicago.
By the end, Middlemarch *no longer*
separated us. Her warm breasts
in the dark. Demand what? Maybe
that I not forget, ever, what it is like
in the dark kissing a stranger
with a long black braid, Middlemarch
on her lap. All that amazing
willingness. Maybe what the saints
want from us is that from the heart
of our passion we worship
their calm—not because such calm
will ever be ours, but because
once the bus stops in Chicago,
there will be a world of pain ahead,
and no way for either of us to escape it.

THE WORK OF BEING

Living at the end of an empire
is sometimes bliss. I know love mostly
as an afterthought: the silence that begins
after the twelve deep bells stop ringing.
Someone not so very far away
plays a harpsichord. The world is slow
and yet filled with the busyness of swallows.
It is not so easy being the species that lives
inside time, crying out again and again, desperate
for timelessness. The harpsichord, the swallows,
the doves hoarse with song, the work
of being. A ruler decides his suffering people
should continue in their suffering
unto their end. If I knew how to end
this poem with doves, I would.
If I knew another word for hunger. For empire
near its end. For love. For those twelve bells
ringing out. Then the silence afterward.

FEAR AND LOVE

I wish I could make the argument that a river
and a sunset plus a calm disregard of the ego
are enough. But whatever comes next must include
tents in the parking lot, that homeless camp
on the way to the airport,
and the hole in your cheek
from the cancer removed yesterday.
I said last night
in the few seconds before I fell asleep,
*You do realize, don't you, everything
is falling apart?* You said, *OK,
I'll try to keep that in mind.* And now it is
starting to be late again, just like every other night
for the last seventy-five years. *Fear and love,*
a friend said in an impromptu speech
at his surprise birthday party,
we all live caught between fear and love.
He tried to smile as he spoke, then sat down.
Yesterday you saw the moon
from the operating table
where they were about to cut you.
Look! you demanded, and the surgeon bent and turned
to see it from your angle,
knife in hand.

IT

If the neighbor's roof is a shamble of broken tiles, so be it.

If those tiles sit there for weeks. If no one does a thing about them.

If the sky is gray day after day and snow falls and the tiles turn into fragments of a broken alphabet traced in snow, clinging.

Darkness, then dawn.

If beauty, as hoped for; if death, as promised.

There is no reason not to say it: the woman with her head bent, reading, is beautiful.

The train rocks beneath her, but she mostly sits in stillness.

A slight trembling of the page betrays the truth of things.

Meanwhile, a window above her bent head. A river and a bridge, a sky darkening just beyond the window.

The bridge and the sky, the slight blue of a river: a world beautiful beyond our understanding.

No reason not to say it: the woman will look up from her book, from the calm page, from the story not her own.

In due course, she will suffer before she dies.

The small blue relief of the river is a darkening song without end.

A MOMENT

I was sitting somewhere beautiful, sunlight
and shadow, people walking slowly by.
I was at peace in that simple, uncomplicated way
that so rarely happens. It was just then I heard a man
imitating a dog for laughs, pretending to howl in pain.
He did it again and again, until finally a real dog nearby,
with long, silken flaps for ears, called back to him,
a true howl without irony, long and slow,
in dumb animal brotherhood, one creature
calling out to another in need, the way
any of us might wish we could call out,
at least once in our lives, one to the other.

BY THE LIGHT OF TWO UNDERLYING CONDITIONS

It helps, if you are seventy-seven, to feel shorn,
as an animal might feel shorn, unburdened
of its too-muchness. It helps
if you carry with you, like two candles to light the way,
two underlying conditions by which to see day passing
into darkness.

And it helps to listen to Beethoven's late sonatas.
We are merely the keys: a music beyond
our understanding plays us as it will.

That screened-in porch, not far
from the ocean: it is a summer night
and I am the small boy in the hammock
swaying back and forth, barely awake.
One of my grown-ups carries me inside
after I have fallen asleep. In the morning
it helps to wake to the sound of the waves,
not quite knowing where I am
or why I am there. To what now
do I truly belong? Shall I call them suffering
and joy, my two underlying conditions?

IT IS ALMOST TIME

If we live on earth at all, pith of loneliness.
The belly of the whale.
I am ten, maybe eleven. Hell is a windowless basement
with a room I call mine, above which
the whole house pretends to make merry.
I nail a crude sign—broken piece of wood—
to my door: STAY OUT. Inside that room
I take off my shirt and box against an invisible opponent:
myself.

Seventy years later
there is a three-quarter moon roaming through the city,
all the more amazing
for being dead and risen
at the same time.

We never fully grasp, do we,
the blue and white of it slowly sinking.
Never fully grasp, even by its calm light,
just how difficult our lives are.
That we have mothers who die.
That we have choke holds and even
that they are used. That we never rise again.
If only we could grasp it, how rare it is

to be a life at all.

After the first abandonment we grow more tender
(warning: this may take seventy-five years).
There was a mother who loved us, even
if only for a moment. If we live on earth at all,
we are someone who learns to love,
even if only for a moment.

AT THE LAST FUNERAL ON EARTH

A boy, sitting in the back of the church,

does a magic trick in which the last rabbit

on earth disappears forever.

The minister, sounding like the lost soul

he is about to become, cries and laughs at the same time.

The mourners look at each other with such love

you know right away something is wrong.

The sun shines because it doesn't have a clue.

Truly the last moment is near,

but out of a kindness of which no one knew

they were capable, in the vestry afterward,

people only speak of the weather while they eat

the very last brownies. Meanwhile, outside,

where Main meets Clay, five women talking and laughing

shake their delighted heads at seagulls flying

toward the sea as they will insist on doing

right up to the end. Two small dogs stick two small heads

out of one open car window. It is the day

the butterflies return in their hundreds

to our little town, stopping only briefly

on their way farther south. Later, a woman goes out

for her usual run at dusk even though

she knows what she knows. It is not pathetic.

It is beautiful. Inside the coffee shop,

Main and River, one bearded black man,

and one clean-shaven white guy reach

for the cream at the same time. One planet,

too many stars to count, three small birches

barely visible in last light.

PARADISE

Stumble and rise is the rhythm of paradise, the echo of footsteps at midnight, moonless or moonlit, it doesn't matter.

Paradise requires an old cat sitting by the drain next to the door of the church, her small tongue at the ready, requires the stones of a piazza that have been crumbling forever into dusty rubble.

Paradise is the cat shrinking back into a corner when at midnight two teenagers arrive on a motorbike, the huge cough of the bike's exhaust, their excited laughter, the girl with her arms around the waist of the boy

Paradise is the boy, ready for anything, his helmet resting on its straps in the cradle of his arm, the motor idling, the cat completely still watching the girl from its hiding place as the girl watches the boy.

Paradise: midnight, her arms around his waist, moonless or moonlit.

A YOUNG MAN, A STRANGER, SMILED AT ME

Maybe I reminded him of his grandfather
or his favorite teacher in grade school,
    the one who lied to him
about his painting of the goldfish bowl,
    who looked hard at it and said, *Beautiful*.

THINGS THAT KEEP ME FROM FORGETTING
WHO I AM:

Easter morning. Rain. Bells at 9 a.m. In the empty tomb, the cave, only bats are left: think what they must have seen!

* * *

Sunlight on an old stone wall—that's a story that's been writing itself for many centuries now.

* * *

Everyone is leaving the little park to go home for dinner. It is sweet sometimes to be the one left behind.

* * *

My green hill in the rain. On Easter, its silence feels holy. I even forget to ask myself whether or not I am happy.

* * *

Spring morning: you touch me and I touch you.

*

. . . and the day after I died,
twilight was especially
beautiful, the mix
of light and its going away
on the river, the way
one led to the other.
The day after,
there were still old men
out walking their dogs
in last light. The dogs were
as excited as always.
The morning after I died,
you studied Italian in bed, as
always. Not a cloud
in the sky. The word
for the day is pensare.
The example is, "Don't
think too much." You
smile at that. You
think too much. That
night, at twilight, tell
me you walked by
the river.

POEM THAT LEAVES BEHIND THE OCEAN

1

I've always wanted to write a poem that ends
at the ocean. How the poem gets there
doesn't much matter, just so at last
it arrives. The manatee will be there
we saw all those years ago,
almost motionless under the water
like a pendant swaying at an invisible throat,
the one my mother used to wear
on the most special of occasions. My God
is still there, the one I prayed to as a boy:
he never answered but that didn't keep me
from calling out to him.

2

I turn off the notification app for good,
no longer needing to know exactly how many gone.
After all, clinging to life
is what we have always done best.
We are still trying to hide
from the truth of things and who
can blame us.
Lists don't make sense anymore,
unless toilet paper and peanut butter head them.
Last-stage patients are not being told
how crowded the ferry will be
that will take them across the river.

3

We are forbidden cafés, churches, even cemeteries.
Fishing by ourselves, however, is still permitted. As long
as we keep nothing at all. As long as we walk
back home, in darkness, empty-handed,
breathing deeply, having thrown back
what was never ours to keep.

EVEN IN THESE TIMES

A man in work clothes checks the meter outside the parking lot.
Sunlight makes a run for it at 5:45 a.m.
A young man wears a cap backwards and walks a dog.
Even now, inspiration, more often than not,
leads nowhere. I continue to not believe in joy,
but it believes in me and arrives, right on time, all
dressed in black, as if for a funeral, perched
on the wing of a crow covered in sunlight.

The ecstasy now

is simply my hand scratching my head
underneath what is left of my hair
and noticing the rolled cuffs—plaid—
of the man exiting the parking lot.
Or "the man existing the parking lot,"
as I just mistakenly wrote.
There is ecstasy sometimes in intending
exiting, but writing *existing*.
Certainly the ecstasy now is the simple pigeon
flying through the simple sky
and my simply being able to see it.
It's the blue car,
the red car, and all the rest
of the revving motors lined up
inside my heart: that they so want
to race until the end of time.
The ecstasy now
is the gray day growing grayer.
It's even diabetes
with its bloody little pricks
delivering the glucose news.
And it's that woman over there
in the billowing dress
on the purple bicycle, deciding
at the last minute to turn left
into traffic, and still, she lives.

It is the stooped-over man
with the wide-brimmed, too-heavy hat
in that Japanese movie,
the old black-and-white one.
He goes to the doctor and overhears, by accident,
he has seventy days left; seventy-five tops. God knows

what gets into him, but he finds
a shovel and a rake and makes
a little neighborhood park by poking around
under some old trees, I don't remember, maybe oaks,
maybe ancient maples. But big ones, trees that understand
how to dignify the little world of his neighborhood.
Day after day, the scratching and digging. The rearranging.
He lives long enough to stand under those trees,
when finally the park is done. It is December now,
day falling into darkness, big hat in hand,
snow slowly descending all around him,
those fluffy flakes that only fall
in that dreamy way in movies.
Isn't now the time to pick up your shovel and start?

USELESS SHOVEL

It is not easy trying to make peace
with the fact that I am one of the lesser ones.

How exactly is that supposed to work?
I know I love this February blizzard

as much as anyone. So that is something.
And Sally, who has lost all language

and smiles out of habit, not pleasure
or understanding, Sally is not lesser:

if there is a God, Sally sits with her silence
at that God's table. One way to see it

is that Sally and I are somehow partners,
like this blizzard and its man in an orange vest,

carrying a shovel, walking through it.
I can assure you, that shovel is completely useless

in this unending snow. How beautiful he is, though,
that man walking through falling-snow-light,

carrying over his shoulder his useless shovel.

MILK AND BEANS

Someone in the café says,
"But he's fucking seventy years old!"
A table away I overhear it
and smile my silent fucking smile.
Across the street,
they are making a stage set
as they do every morning
at 7 a.m. I see palm trees
and two crossed swords.
A desert is implied. An oasis.
It is time, once again,
to begin.
Passing my face
in the mirror, I raise one eyebrow,
You devil you,
then head out to buy the milk and beans.

METROPOLITAN DIARY

for JoAnn

There's the entry from June 7, 2020.
A guy remembers 1969, at 9 p.m., Columbus Circle, Miles Davis pulls up
    next to him, nods,
and speeds away in a yellow roadster, top down.

The one when it is 1962,
June night, third shift, and I lean against the grain bags
in Building Four looking out at the night sky: oh, the bliss
of third shift at nineteen, silence and stars, no end to anything in sight.

The one when it is May 28, 2020,
and sitting at my window watching the young march past in masks. They
    are calling out, *Justice.*
They are calling out, *Say his name.*

The one when it is 2030 and I am long gone
and the full moon rises over the park while a young family sits there
in moony darkness and does not mind that I remind them,
from a far distance, that happiness and melancholy
need not see each other as enemies.

The one in 2021 when I am still alive
and it is June again and dark. Someone I love will turn seventy-one in
    two days
and I will look over and nod the way Miles Davis did all those years ago:
and when I pull away at some still unspecified time (because such departures
do happen), you will remain behind and say to yourself,
Did that really happen! and, *Was that really him?* And, *Isn't it crazy*
that my heart broke open, both in joy and sadness? That I lived?

June 9, 2020, Minneapolis

THE SITUATION

A lit cross in last light, shining down
from somewhere far away, the smell of pigs
being pigs. There was a situation to which
they all belonged, not entirely clear, but theirs,
and they pretended to be grown-up about it,
but really, it allowed for no relief.

                                                At some point,
since he was the oldest, he stood and the others
followed suit. Outside, the new dog
half-heartedly chased the cat,
then stopped to bark at the people one by one
as they stepped into the darkness,
just fallen. The man went off by himself,
behind the house, where a small contingent
of fireflies had begun to light the way.
He loved his people and they loved him.
Hopeless situations had become his specialty:
how to reveal them to those for whom hope
remained a way forward. He returned
and brought them news of the fireflies,
how they give the darkness a shape,
like a sieve of stars, a few feet above earth,
through which darkness pours. It is hardly
a consolation, but it is all he has to offer,
a slurry of small pulsing lights in tall grass
at dusk. Call it beauty and you wouldn't be wrong.
Of course, beauty in and of itself
has never been enough. Ridiculous
to speak of fireflies and tall grasses at such a time.
The situation calls for more than he can give.
The sweet dog barks and barks. It is her way of being kind.

HOME

I came home to the rain.
To the ladder in the rain propped against a steel pipe and leading
    nowhere.
I came home to your cough, to a seagull buried alive in fog, crying out.
I came home to the crying out.
And under the earth, a train shook and groaned carrying people
    through the darkness.
I came home to being carried through darkness.
Each moment was the last moment, each breath my last breath.
I knew my place and my place was resting my head against the ladder
    leading nowhere.

I came home to the statue of the Buddha and said—as if I had a right—
    I want that calm.
How to help but want it?

Came home to Fra Angelico's half-naked man at the foot of the Cross.
How careful he is, as he lowers, inch by inch, the dead Christ into
    our earth.

All those years ago, on her way out the door, mother holding up her
    hand for me to fasten tight her shiny bracelet.

I came home to a feather
tied to the willow by the river as the little darkness of a dove
flew by. I saw that. And then saw those three deer
drinking from the river, looking up suddenly,
remembering they were wild. Remembering now, the last smile
I ever saw on my mother's face.
Rest quietly and wait, my child. You will be called.

THINGS THAT KEEP ME FROM FORGETTING WHO I AM:

That was a different time. Fifteen, in love for the first time, running down the street at midnight from her house to mine.

* * *

The farmer and I greet each other on the empty road and smile because why not?

* * *

The new leaves in spring are singing, "I did it my way."

* * *

And now the little night boat. Leaning over the star railing, I make a wish that I love like a man who knows how to sail.

* * *

I have Giotto's six beautiful faces in the Uffizi. And I have this moment lying with you in bed, our faces so close they make a world, and I have Lake Trasimeno seen from the train window, blue and gray and a weedy green, colors not to be believed. No, not to be believed. And yet, here they are.

* * *

That man with the two nervous greyhounds who walks them late at night—such beautiful creatures, like willow trees given legs—is tonight walking them under the newest of long silver greyhound moons. Two greyhounds under the new moon, trembling.

*

. . . and this strange moment
at night as I drive
the road along the river—
even now at my age, now when
I understand how we live
in a country
always preparing
ground zero somewhere
for someone other—
even now the flickering lights
on both sides of the river
as I drive the bridge,
that breathing darkness
which flowing water makes of itself,
how the sound of the crickets
has all my life
tried to guide me between
dusk fade and dawn rise,
beginning and end,
carrying me far out
beyond myself.

LITTLE SAINTHOOD

On one of my good days
you could tell I lived happily here, inside
the all of it.
You could feel the stillness,
calm as the warm hand
of my father in those few moments
after he died thirty years ago.

On one of my good days
the chipped light that halos
gather to themselves
in the early Renaissance paintings
sheltered me
and I'd think of the end
of both happiness and sadness,
how they must surely collide
in that little moment
before the final one.

The saints' halos mean beauty
and death have made—
against all odds—
a life together. In this sense
we all have our moments
of little sainthood, riding home
in the back seat of the car at age seven,
someone we love
in spite of everything
at the wheel, and a sky
with new darkness pulling down
its curtain over the long double row
of elms, still unsickened
the way they were sixty years ago,
pulling it down easily.

None of this is to imply that life—
in all its thousand wrinkled leaves—
will not go on and on
after someone leaves, having been given,
on one of his good days,
the all of it.

NOW AND THEN

Now it is not like *then*,
though then, too, one day in spring the swifts
suddenly appeared again above the bridge,
rising and falling like stones briefly lost
to gravity: if the air could sing
this would be its song. Then, too, as now,
I could imagine I might join the swifts
the way a wish for a thing can join that thing
as its attendant spirit,
always longing for more.

Then, none of us had a clue
about the masked loneliness
to come. Now, too, the bridge is still
harbored by its swifts.

In a few minutes
I will walk there, and they will also
harbor me, not because they love me or even take
any notice of me at all, but simply because
they are life and I am life, and as it was then, so it is now.

I'D LIKE TO SAY THIS AS CLEARLY AS POSSIBLE

I live in a world in which 5 a.m. moonlight shines down on an empty
    parking lot.
I live in a world in which rain falls on the bridge at noon. In which
    loneliness
is never lonely for company.
As clearly as possible I'd like to say:
my soul is as plain as a fallen leaf on a sidewalk—as useless, and as
    beautiful.

MINNEAPOLIS

Well, we sat in the darkness, lights out.
Knowing the river is nearby. Knowing the bluffs.
The smell of the lindens.

As the darkness deepened, a new smell of burning tires, of stores
    smoldering.
"Well," I said, "Maybe tonight there will be peace at last."
Only minutes later, they came by, the protesters.
I wanted to walk with them. But the virus made me afraid.

I sat at the window and watched the young pass by.
Did they see an old man sitting there, looking at them?
Well, their signs, hand-printed:
"I can't breathe," they said, "Murder." "Justice."

We went to bed, watched men and women on TV speaking Italian:
they were hunting the Mafia, being murdered by the Mafia,
wanting to be the Mafia.
Two people in love were walking near the sea on TV.
It was silly. It was only make-believe. We grew sleepy.
Then many dreams. Often waking through the night.

* * *

There was a life I would have gladly lived
to the end: the one of moonlight
and holding on as long as possible to earth
as I had always believed it to be,
no questions asked. Instead,
this. It no longer works now to live
one life at a time. No, nor one death.

Sometimes I'm a million miles away
from myself. I'm happiest then, not being
anyone I know all that well. Sometimes
I simply sit at home, my face unmasked, naked.
I look out the window. I note sunlight
and rain. Last night, a little shoehorn
of a moon, just as queenly as if
none of this was happening.

           At sunrise
my heart lifted a bit like a curtain
rising on a play I'd heard might be worth
the trouble. An eagle flew by with a fish in its talons.
We opened the window. The sounds of sirens again.
The full-throated horns of fire trucks. Helicopters overhead.
The war had begun yet again. I could end here. But, well,

I am seventy-seven, have no time to waste.
It is time for me too, even now, to begin again.

PROGNOSIS

      I watch an old man with a plastic sack
walk backward in the February wind,
      his face turned away
from the worst of it.
      I'm fine, thank you
very much, but
      there is a part of me—
I can admit this now—
      that is waiting to die.
And strangely, the waiting
      goes well:

February sunlight
      and an empty road
lined with trees.
      Meanwhile,
my friend
      who can no longer speak,
pointing at the picture
      of the artichoke,
smiles knowingly.

I WILL STILL BE HERE

I know I call in a time of great sadness and anger,
in a time of such fear: still,
if you can manage to answer
we might talk into the long winter night.
I will still be here when the lights on the bridge
go out and the pink flash at dawn disappears,
when the geranium's single flower bends over double
under the weight of its own blossoming.

THINGS THAT KEEP ME FROM FORGETTING WHO I AM:

The sky filled with thousands of floating fluff puffs, frail as sleeping faces in a hospital, but filled with sunlight. We are all in it together, after all.

* * *

Blue mountains in the distance. If my mother had told me, even once, that she loved me . . . if I had told her even once . . .

* * *

Made something of a fool of myself last night at dinner, shouting at my deaf friend while looking unabashedly at that woman at the other end of the table.

* * *

I would have been kinder had I known what was coming.

* * *

If it happens that I must die with a tyrant in office, then it is even more important to say that I see the mint plant blazing in sunlight.

* * *

Lilacs already, and a man with so much of everything bends toward them as if he has nothing.

*

WHERE IT TAKES ME

To the olive grove past Bassano, and the blue-gray smudge
of the hill beyond, like smoke from a fire that won't stop burning.

      To a dead man called Christ, and daisies near his gray face,
      anonymous painter, Byzantine, first floor in the Accademia.

To the look on Lida's face when she told us how the fascists
dragged her father from the house, made her watch as they shot him.

      Near wild roses along the railroad tracks in St. Paul
      where Dale Street begins to leave the city.

Near wild roses, anywhere.

      To that boy in Iraq, lying on a mattress, crying,
      his father dead for no reason save us.

The back seat of the car, the day after Easter, watching five gray nuns
walk slowly through the failing light up the cathedral stairs toward God.

      To these blackest of crows calling out from the broken branch
          on top of the almond tree,
      blossoms come and gone. As if a god is crying out within, all
          beauty fled.

To you, little girl, standing under the cypress just past the town
    cemetery, waving
as I drove past so quickly I never noticed how short life is.

      To sleep with its dreams and then, waking, again into history.
      To death and the hope for God, and, for God's sake, to Filippo
          Lippi, to beauty.

To the strangers in search of beauty, that is, to us in need,
to our desperation, how unending, how necessary.

> To smoke on the hill at dawn and the white road that leads
> nowhere, empty as always.
> To the way things disappear without a trace, each time taking
> me with them.

ACKNOWLEDGMENTS

Friendships and professional support have been important to me as I wrote these poems. Much of *Prognosis* was written during the last four years, a time of lockdown and societal trauma. These editors and their publications helped create a path for me through the isolation of this period:

Sven Birkerts at Agni Online for "The Problem"
André Naffis-Sahely at *Ambit* for "Today's Meditation"
Catherine Segurson at *Catamaran* for "In the Poems I Love"
Kathleen Kirk at *Escape into Life* for "The ecstasy now," "Instead,"
  "It Is Almost Time," "Little Sainthood," "Milk and Beans,"
  "That man running," and "Useless Shovel"
Mark Drew at the *Gettysburg Review* for "Where It Takes Me"
David Baker at the *Kenyon Review* for "I call it joy," "It," and
  "Not to Know How to Live"
Kevin Young (and Hannah Aizenman) at the *New Yorker* for
  "Poem that Leaves Behind the Ocean" (as "Poem that
  Ends at the Ocean") and "Whatever Else"
Darren Morris at *Parhelion* for the eight columnar poems
  beginning with the word "And"
Vijay Seshadri at the *Paris Review* for "Admit It"
Danny Lawless at *Plume* magazine for "Driving the River Road"
  and "Prognosis"
Susan Solomon, Todd Pederson, and Jamie Lynn Buehner
  at *Sleet* for "Paradise," "Transfiguration from the Li Po,"
  "At the Last Funeral on Earth," "By the Light of Two
  Underlying Conditions," and "Last Day at Seventy-Five"
Alice Quinn, editor of the anthology *Together in a Sudden
  Strangeness: America's Poets Respond to the Pandemic* for
  "Cheese, Almonds, Eggs"
Sarah Byrne at the *Well Literary Review* for "Greed"

In addition, the Academy of American Poets' *Poem-a-Day* for
  "My Bracelet"

I want to thank everyone at Graywolf Press for supporting and nurturing this book. Fiona McCrae has been there for me and for my work for almost two decades. Her presence has made all the difference. I keep trying, unsuccessfully, to find the right words with which to thank her so that she might have some understanding of the enormous gratitude I feel.

I was lucky to have two brilliant editors for this book: Jeff Shotts in its very early stages and Chantz Erolin who has guided the editorial process throughout. His eagle eye, unending patience, and open heart have been all that I could have hoped for.

In addition I want to thank, for their support of my work as a poet during the time of the writing of this book, my sister Madeline and Michael Dennis Browne, Margaret Fulton, Margaret Hasse, Jane Hilberry, Jane Hirshfield, Marie Howe, Jane Hilberry, Deborah Keenan, Gretchen Marquette, Carol Moldaw, Alice Quinn, Holly Wren Spaulding, Arthur Sze, JoAnn Verburg, and Jay White.

JoAnn Verburg is the light of my life.

JIM MOORE is the author of seven previous books of poetry. His work has appeared in the *American Poetry Review*, the *Antioch Review*, *Harper's Magazine*, the *Kenyon Review*, the *Nation*, the *New Yorker*, the *Paris Review*, *Sleet*, *Water-Stone Review*, and many other magazines, as well as in two editions of the *Pushcart Prize Anthology*. The poem "For You" was also reprinted in *The Pushcart Book of Poetry*. An excerpt of his poem "Love in the Ruins" appeared in New York subways and buses as part of the Poetry Society of America's Poetry in Motion initiative. He is the recipient of fellowships from the Bush Foundation, the Jerome Foundation, the McKnight Foundation, the Minnesota State Arts Board, and most recently the Guggenheim Foundation. Moore has taught in various universities and colleges, most recently in the MFA program at Hamline University in Saint Paul, Minnesota, and Colorado College in Colorado Springs. He and his wife, the photographer JoAnn Verburg, live in Minneapolis and in Spoleto, Italy.

The text of *Prognosis* is set in Adobe Caslon Pro.
Book design by Rachel Holscher.
Composition by Bookmobile Design and Digital
Publisher Services, Minneapolis, Minnesota.
Manufactured by Friesens on acid-free,
100 percent postconsumer wastepaper.